the Participation Playbook

Three Ways Smart Managers Make Work Better for All

MOLLY BREAZEALE

A PREAMBLE

I AM A PARTICIPATION EVANGELIST

———

MY PHILOSOPHY. The workplace provides individuals (beyond just a paycheck) with an identity, a community, and the potential for mastery of their God-given gifts.

MY BELIEF. Managers make that possible in their daily interactions with individuals and teams by linking who they are with what they do in personally meaningful ways.

MY INTENTION. These pages are to be read and internalized for personal meaning and then put into practice through the development of this playbook, which is designed as a call to action.

YOUR PARTICIPATION. By allowing your hopes and challenges to be reflected in the pages that follow, you'll be able to create a playbook that makes work better for all. Your participation matters.

WELCOME

I'M GLAD YOU ARE HERE

The notice inside my paycheck read something like this: The employees at Delta Air Lines would like to buy their company a Boeing-767. Would you like to contribute? Although the rest of this notice went into more detail, I paused and carefully decided to do my part. As a young flight attendant, I knew the airline industry was troubled by a weak economy, high fuel prices, and deregulation. My friends at Eastern Airlines had warned me about this as they had received multiple pay cuts without notice.

Delta's approach was different. Delta was not making a critical decision for me. They made it my choice to participate in the purchase of the Boeing-767 and to determine how much and over what period of time I'd like my automatic payroll deductions to occur.

I'll never forget the day *The Spirit of Delta* rolled out of the hangar. With tears in my eyes, I felt a deep emotional connection and commitment to the organization. Etched in my memory, that inspiring moment set my career in motion in leadership and talent development.

Thirty years ago, I read a book by Fran Rees entitled *How to Lead Work Teams: Facilitation Skills* (1991). I highlighted and underlined the following passage for it captured my experience at Delta Airlines in words that became my mantra and guiding belief: **"people support what they help create, and decisions are best made at the levels where they will be carried out"** (p. 2).

As a manager, you are not alone. Without compromising quality or investing too much time and energy, you can release the untapped potential of everyone on your team through the power of participation.

Managing from the middle is hard. You have a tremendous responsibility yet an incredible opportunity to make a difference in your life and the life of those you lead.

Let's get started!

———

Molly Breazeale

THE PARTICIPATION COACH

PARTICIPATION

PARTICIPATION: Turn thoughts and feelings into action.

IMAGINE IT.

What if everyone on your team knew how they contributed to the organization, felt free to work in ways that played to their strengths, and could recognize progress toward personally meaningful goals?

You, as a manager, can make that happen.

THINK ABOUT IT.

Businesses and individuals want to realize their full potential; develop it in the most efficient, effective way; and measure progress over time. It's time to rethink daily interactions as a manager and pivot from being the "sage on the stage to the guide on the side," creating organizational clarity, team alignment, and individual support to make work better for all.

CREATE IT.

You realize the untapped potential at your fingertips yet struggle to unleash it. Operational goals and unrealistic time pressures overshadow relationship-building and clear, consistent communication. It's isolating, exhausting, and frustrating.

The best learning and development come from working on real business problems together.

But it's easier and faster to react and do things yourself than to reflect on who really should be making the decision and identifying what resources they need to make it.

That's why you need a playbook.

THE PLAYBOOK

THE PLAYBOOK: A Plan to create meaningful work experiences.

What is a playbook?

For the time-strapped, can't-be-everywhere manager like you, this tool provides core, common, and consistent communication in one designated location. Playbooks can be a simple document, a slide deck, or a webpage with shared documents that are stored and updated for easy access.

Playbooks create the foundation to connect people to each other and to the work, helping everyone stay focused, organized, and accountable to each other for results.

What's the purpose of a playbook?

Although organizations focus on data and information to drive strategy, operations, and performance, individuals want the experience of being trusted, valued, and recognized for doing their part. It's time to rethink daily communication to link who we are with what we do in personally meaningful ways.

Through the power of participation, smart managers bridge the communication gap between business needs and the human need for emotional connection. That task requires a new, more proactive approach to the daily experience of work as well as a change in perspective.

What's included in this playbook?

Designing for an emotional connection requires a different approach than merely sharing business information, timelines, and directives. As a manager, what you say and what you do set the tone for individual relationships and the well-being of the work environment.

By creating this playbook, you'll have a plan that includes three ways to make work better for all:

1. **Create a sense of PURPOSE.** Create organizational clarity so everyone experiences a sense of purpose.

2. **PARTICIPATE as a partner.** Build team alignment, freeing individuals to play to their strengths for efficiency and effectiveness.

3. **Make PROGRESS possible.** Recognize and support individuals as they strive to achieve personally meaningful goals.

THE PROCESS

Slice open an apple, and you'll find seeds for growth at the core. Given the right environment, those seeds release future potential, produce fruit, and multiply.

Smart Managers Know You Reap What You Sow

While it's simpler to call people together and tell them clearly what to do, it is not effective in the long run.

– Brian Stanfield, *The Art of Focused Conversation* (2009)

BELIEFS DRIVE ACTIONS

Human beings are meaning-making machines. Looking at daily interactions through a personal lens, they decide, "what does this mean to me?"

From onboarding a new employee to monitoring daily performance, meaningful work is doing your part to solve business challenges together, allowing people to be informed, involved, and inspired to do their best work.

We rely on data to tell us what happened and stories to tell us what it means.

– Nancy Duarte, *DataStory: Explain Data and Inspire Action Through Story* (2019)

Data is fundamental to good decision-making and provides a path to the future, but data is data and has little value until human beings give it meaning. Whenever we take information in through the senses, we experience an internal response. In other words, we process new information by telling stories about what it means to us based on our experience.

Meaning isn't a decision to act. Action is a whole-body experience of head, heart, and guts. For example, you may know you need to lose weight and feel committed to your goals until dinner with friends or the need for a reward after a long week derails your best intentions.

Relationships and the physical environment sit at the heart of human decision-making. The stories we tell ourselves about who we are and what we are willing to do are internally focused on risk and reward.

THERE IS NO SUBSTITUTE FOR EXPERIENCE.

Meaningful work is a personal choice. People want to know they matter to those around them and that their work makes a difference. As a manager, the best use of your time and effort is to create experiences that inform, involve, and inspire individuals to apply their God-given gifts to business challenges and opportunities.

It's a law of human nature that people commit to a decision in proportion to the extent they feel they participated in making it. As a result of their participation, they build confidence and self-esteem by doing hard things together and discovering what works.

Your roadmap for developing this playbook is to apply the CORE methodology to the following pages. It's designed to turn your thoughts and feelings about the world of work into actions you are willing to take to create meaningful experiences for all.

What We Believe Is How We Behave

MEANING-MAKING = thoughts and beliefs about what change is needed (head and heart).

DECISION-MAKING = a personal choice to act based on the current conditions (guts).

Stories Turn Data and Information Into Meaningful Participation

MEANING-MAKING: Stories We Tell Ourselves About What Is Happening and Why

C

CONTEXT: Meet people where they are.

What is happening in the workplace today?

Based on your experience, what do these changes mean to you?

O

OUTCOMES: Define expected outcomes for the future.

What is the gap between current conditions and desired future performance?

What needs to change for managers to close the gap?

DECISION-MAKING: Stories That Determine What We Are Willing To Do as a Result

R

RELATIONSHIPS: Give everyone a role to play.

What would these changes look like and sound like for you to create opportunities for meaningful participation?

E

ENVIRONMENT: Determine what resources and conditions are needed.

What would you need to succeed if you were in their shoes?

What barriers or obstacles exist?

The future Abraham Maslow describes in his journals is the world we live in today—the digital age. A world in which human potential will be the primary source of competitive advantage.

CONTEXT

CONTEXT: Begin by understanding where you are.

What is happening in the world of work? What does it mean to you?

The internet differs from most of the mass media it replaces in an obvious and very important way: it's bidirectional.

– Nicholas Carr, The Shallows: What the Internet Is Doing to Our Brains (2020)

In recent years, list some of the devices your smartphone has replaced:

No plan survives its collision with reality.

– Susan Scott, Fierce Conversations (2002)

When Conditions Change, Relationships Change

THE POWER SHIFT

Whenever we encounter an external reality, we experience an internal response. In other words, we process new data and information by determining what it means to us. Those beliefs then guide our actions.

MORE OPTIONS, MORE CONTROL

For example, banking used to be conducted at a physical location with specific hours of operation. When we interacted and how much effort it took to complete a transaction was controlled by the institution. Today, consumers can bank at their convenience—anytime and anywhere. We can point to countless other examples of external forces changing behavior and expectations.

CONTROL OR CREATE

Consider the difference between a remote-control device and a smartphone as an analogy for this power shift. The remote is designed for control and one-directional communication. In contrast, the smartphone is bidirectional, providing unlimited opportunities to connect and create, setting a new standard for expectations in how and when we work together.

TABLE 1. PAST AND FUTURE CONDITIONS	
Past Conditions	**Future Conditions**
Work 9 to 5	Work anytime
Work in a corporate office	Work anywhere
Use company equipment	Use any device
Climb the corporate ladder	Create a personal ladder
Connect to one device	Connect to multiple devices

Conditions Changed, Relationships Changed

A survey by Microsoft 2022 Work Trend Index found that 41% of the workforce is considering leaving their job in the coming year, the biggest reason being **unsustainable workloads.**

The U.S. Department of Labor and other major workforce surveys indicate that the **Great Resignation** continues and is about far more than just the workload. It's personal.

When work may be at the kitchen table or in a corner of the bedroom, personal lives enter into the mix in ways never experienced before. One colleague remarked, "I'm not working from home; I'm living at work."

According to a survey by Ernst Young (Ernst & Young, 2022), **54% of workers left** a previous job **because their boss wasn't empathetic** to their struggles at work, and **49% said employers were unsympathetic to their personal lives.**

Burnout in managers increased from 27% in 2020 to 35% in 2021, according to a November 2021 Gallup report.

I Will is more important than IQ.

—Kathy Kolbe, The Conative Connection: Uncovering the Link Between Who You Are and How You Perform (1990)

Today, more and more workers are worried about making ends meet, dealing with chronic stress, and struggling to balance the demands of both work and personal lives. The toll on their mental health is growing.

The pandemic also sparked a reckoning among many workers who no longer feel that sacrificing their health, family, and communities for work is an acceptable trade-off.

Organizations are also increasingly aware of the trade-off; when the mental health of workers suffers, so does workplace productivity, creativity, and retention.

—Dr. Vicek H. Murthy M.D., M.B.A., The U.S. Surgeon General's Framework for Workplace Mental Health and Well-Being (2022)

The Meaning of Work
in a Smartphone World

MEANING-MAKING = thoughts and beliefs about what change is needed (head and heart).

Pause. Take a moment to reflect.

1. EXTERNAL REALITY

What conditions have changed the most in your workplace?

What do those changes mean to you?

- ☐ When? (email, text, expectations)
- ☐ Where? (hybrid office, deskless environment, corner of the bedroom or kitchen table)
- ☐ How? (technology, balancing with caregiving roles, multiple jobs, the gig economy)

2. INTERNAL RESPONSE

In what ways has this changed the manager-employee relationship?

- ☐ Communication
- ☐ Role expectations
- ☐ Decision rights
- ☐ Career development
- ☐ Other ways

3. THE POWER SHIFT FOR MANAGERS

Based on your experience, what should change for managers to make work better for all?

Management is an intervention more like bridge-building than rain dancing: there is a cause-effect relationship between a manager's actions and an employee's performance.

– Ferdinand Fournies, Why Employees Don't Do What They Are Supposed to Do and What to Do About It (2007)

Behaviors are beliefs turned into action. Behaviors deliver the results. They're where the rubber meets the road.

– Larry Bossidy and Ram Charan, Execution: The Discipline of Getting Things Done (2002)

DECISION-MAKING = a personal choice to act based on
the current conditions (guts).

Pause. Take a moment to reflect.

4. RELATIONSHIPS

Pull out your calendar and identify your next team meeting.
For the outcomes listed below, what can you **say or do** to create these conditions for meaningful work:

- ☐ **Create a sense of PURPOSE.** Create organizational clarity so everyone experiences a sense of purpose.
- ☐ **PARTICIPATE as a partner.** Build team alignment, freeing individuals to play to their strengths for efficiency and effectiveness.
- ☐ **Make PROGRESS possible.** Recognize and support individuals as they strive to achieve personally meaningful goals.

5. ENVIRONMENT

What would you need to succeed if you were in their shoes?
What barriers or obstacles exist?

6. WHEN CONDITIONS CHANGE, RELATIONSHIPS CHANGE.

Only the leader can set the tone of the dialogue in the organization. ***Dialogue is the core of culture and the basic unit of work.***

How people talk to each other absolutely determines how well the organization will function.

OUTCOMES

OUTCOMES: Identify what needs to change.

What can you do to improve the workplace experience?

Managing from the middle, primarily responsible for strategy implementation, you must now have your finger on the pulse of the employee experience, creating an environment where people want to invest their time and best efforts to grow the business and develop their God-given talents and skills.

Change Your Perspective:
What You Believe Is How You Behave

In his 2021 article, "Work Is Still Work," Josh Bersin says, "People come to work to express and share their God-given gifts with others. Give them the opportunity and freedom to do this, and they'll do amazing things." As a manager, it takes courage and humility to act on this belief in what you say and do, but the results can be transformational.

You Have More Power Than You Think

Being the face of decisions you didn't make, reacting to urgent last-minute demands, and trying to protect team members who are already stretched thin is a recipe for manager burnout and defeat. This is not sustainable and creates a challenging environment for all.

Change the Conversation: What You Say and Do Are Employee Experiences

Although you can't do much to control the directives from senior leadership or timelines and outcomes imposed, you can change the way you prepare and participate in daily conversations by linking who you are to what you do in personally meaningful ways.

It starts with a pivot from being the "sage on the stage to the guide on the side." Professor Alison King, College of Education at California State University, used that phrase to describe the typical lecture: "The professor is the central figure (sage) and transmits knowledge to the student, assuming their brain is an empty container." Ouch! No one wants that experience.

Dialogue Is the Core of Culture and the Basic Unit of Work

Integrating the business need for performance with individual needs for experiences that free employees to develop their full potential is both an art and a science.

The heart of a business is how the three processes of people, strategy, and operations link together.

—Larry Bossidy and Ram Charan,

Execution: The Discipline of Getting Things Done (2002)

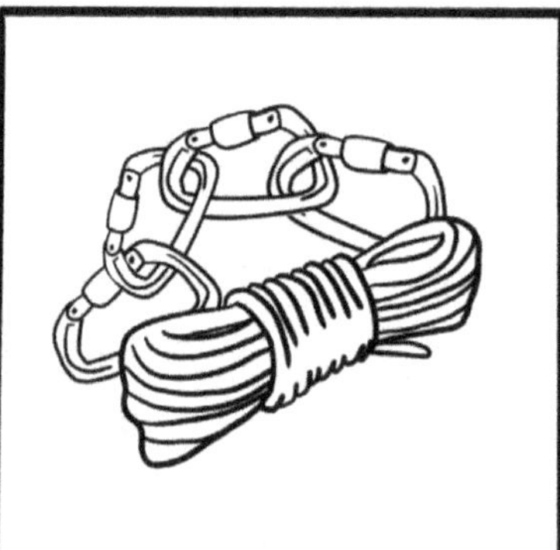

The Art and Science
of Performance Conversations

Consider a mountain-climbing expedition as an analogy for two points of view about performance, with these definitions taken from the *Mountaineering: The Freedom of the Hills*, 8th ed. (2010):

- **Orientation:** the science of determining your exact position on the Earth
- **Navigation:** the science of determining the location of your objective and staying pointed in the right direction from the starting point to the destination
- **Route-Finding:** the art of selecting and following the best path appropriate for the abilities and equipment of the climbing party

ORIENTATION

BUSINESS PERSPECTIVE:

Planning a mountain-climbing expedition requires determining which mountain to climb, why that mountain, and allocating resources for a successful venture. Mission statements, visions of the future, and values provide employees with purpose and direction for an organization's journey, focusing everyone's time and energy on reaching the summit.

INDIVIDUAL PERSPECTIVE:

Clarity about the mission and understanding of the role provides individuals with a sense of identity and purpose. Individuals choose to be contributing members of the expedition, where they can realize their potential.

NAVIGATION

BUSINESS PERSPECTIVE:

Once the mountain-climbing expedition is defined, organizing the timing, sequence, and resources needed to reach the summit is the next step, just like the business decisions made to manage resources for efficiency and effectiveness.

Within the hierarchy, systems, and processes designed to ensure long-term success, managers provide clear direction and rationale for the decisions made. Working in partnership across the organization, they share goals, objectives, and resources with others to stay on track.

INDIVIDUAL PERSPECTIVE:

Aligning individual talents best suited for the tasks builds efficiency, effectiveness, and communities where people feel trusted and valued for their unique contributions, whether scaling a mountain or an ERP implementation.

Participating in the decisions needed to organize efforts, timelines, and resources allows individuals to freely choose to support those decisions with the freedom to do their best work.

ROUTE-FINDING

BUSINESS PERSPECTIVE:

Safety and security are job number one for leaders of a mountain-climbing expedition. Selecting and following the best path requires recognizing the abilities of each team member, securing the necessary equipment, and creating the conditions that allow every individual to do their best work. This is more art than science.

INDIVIDUAL PERSPECTIVE:

For a climb to be safe and successful, everyone leads. Team members must depend on each other to solve problems, make decisions, and act in everyone's best interests. Managers like you must create the right conditions for peer-to-peer learning, competing points of view, and the safety of speaking freely.

Developing mastery of talents and skills is a process that takes place over time. In his earliest works, Abraham Maslow said, "Apparently, growth forward takes place in little steps, and each step forward is made possible by the feeling of being safe, operating out into the unknown from a safe home port, of daring because retreat is possible."

Understand Your Power Source

Information and position used to be a manager's power source. Today, true power comes from the untapped potential of the team. With the internet in their pocket and a vast array of ideas and experiences, individuals are eager and expect greater opportunities to participate in problem-solving and decision-making. In the experience economy, your employees are the brand.

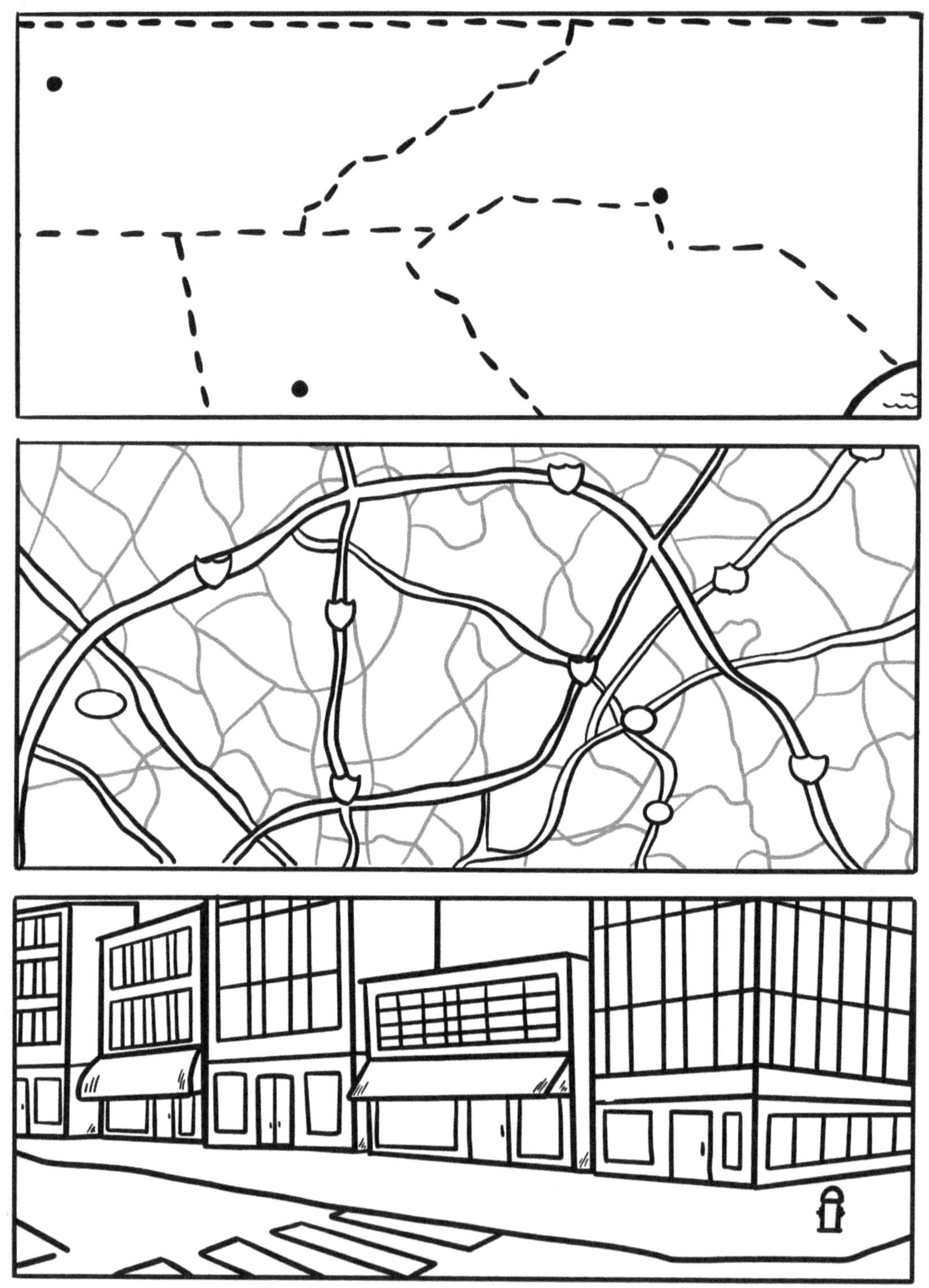

Meaningful Conversations: Purpose, Participation, Progress

Wouldn't it be great to have a Google Maps tool for business meetings and conversations? Just as we can view a map from multiple views or perspectives, the same is true for meetings and conversations.

ORGANIZATIONAL CONVERSATIONS:

Purpose and Direction

You know that most business meetings and conversations are designed and delivered to meet the needs of the business. Business needs generally fall into two areas. Although that's great for determining the direction and coordination between departments, it isn't easy to translate these topics into the tasks needed to complete them. Employees experience a lack of clarity, misalignment, assumptions, and misunderstandings.

TABLE 2. BUSINESS NEEDS	
Reduce Expenses	**Increase Revenue**
Types of waste we can reduce:	*Areas for growth:*
• Overproduction	• Market penetration
• Waiting	• Extended geographic regions
• Inventories	• Customer experience
• Defects	• Products and services
• Behaviors	• Bundling solutions
• Transportation	• Partnerships

Smart managers create opportunities to translate these high-level topics into desired performance outcomes, using them as the basis for problem-solving, decision-making, and creating shared accountability for results as teams work together.

Participation and Connection

Like looking at a map of the United States without major routes or highway systems, strategy and high-level discussions leave too much for teams and individuals to interpret. Team conversations become connecting points that form the basis for healthy relationships and alignment. As a result, they require core, common, and consistent frameworks and structures for creating shared responsibility, maximizing individual talents, and utilizing resources.

Meaningful and Measurable Progress

Like stepping from the curb to cross a busy street, taking action comes with a degree of risk and vulnerability. Even when individuals know what is expected of them, and believe they have what they need to accomplish the task, they may lack the courage to move forward. Coaching individuals to Identify these issues and remove barriers can help them draw on their own resources to turn fear and doubt into confident action.

Pause. Take a moment to reflect.

1. PERFORMANCE AND POTENTIAL

Based on your experience, what is the <u>business impact</u> when the following conditions exist?

- ☐ Lack of organizational clarity
- ☐ Lack of team alignment
- ☐ Lack of individual support

2. PERFORMANCE AND POTENTIAL

Based on your experience, what is the <u>individual impact</u> when the following conditions exist?

- ☐ Lack of organizational clarity
- ☐ Lack of team alignment
- ☐ Lack of individual support

Leadership and learning are indispensable to each other.

—John F. Kennedy

Leadership Is Learning, and Learning Is Partnership

You know what you said.

You don't know what they heard.

You know how you would do it.

You don't know if there is a better, faster, more efficient way.

You know if the performance was satisfactory.

You don't know if it was satisfying or meaningful
to the individual or the team.

Although giving answers is easier and faster than asking good questions, it eliminates the personal decision-making process needed to build trust, respect, and commitment to shared goals. Compare notes from leadership and learning experts in the table below.

Smart managers participate in daily conversations as partners, realizing the untapped potential to make better, faster decisions with clarity, alignment, and support.

TABLE 3. LEARNING AND MOTIVATION	
Drive: The Surprising Truth About What Motivates Us by Daniel Pink (2009)	*The Adult Learner: A Neglected Species* by Malcolm Knowles (1973)
This book was written to highlight for leaders the difference between what science knows and what business does. • Motivation 3.0 presumes that human beings want to learn, create, and better the world. **As human beings, we want:** • Autonomy to direct our own lives • Mastery to extend and expand our abilities • Purpose, to make a contribution	*This book, written by a university professor, was an instant hit with adult educators and teachers.* • Adults want some control over the learning experience. They are self-directed and capable of making decisions. • Adults bring a wealth of knowledge and experience to the learning environment. They learn more effectively through guided discussion and problem-solving than through lectures. • Adults learn best when they have a "need" to learn.

If there is any one secret of success, it lies in the ability to get the other person's point of view and see things from that person's angle as well as from your own.

—*Henry Ford*

RELATIONSHIPS

RELATIONSHIPS: Define what these changes would look like and sound like for you.

Sheela Subramanian of Future Forum says, *"We're still in the biggest workplace paradigm shift we're apt to see in our lifetimes, and leaders are feeling the pressure. We can no longer rely on old leadership playbooks and must redesign our way forward."*

Strategic plans and operational goals don't mean much corporately unless we execute them individually. Managers who effectively link who employees are with what they do in personally meaningful ways will rewrite the script for leaders of the future.

The conversation IS the relationship.

—Susan Scott,
Fierce Conversations (2017)

You Are a Strategy Enabler

In your relationship with the business, you provide clear, timely, data-driven information to translate strategy into performance outcomes, using them as the basis for problem-solving, decision-making, and creating shared accountability for results as teams work together.

You Are an Environment Creator

You provide a process or framework to share responsibility, maximize individual talents, and utilize resources in your relationship with the team. You also manage fear and doubt by removing barriers and obstacles to taking action.

TABLE 4. CAUSE-EFFECT RELATIONSHIP		
Leader Actions	**Produce Employee Results**	**Meet Business And Individual Needs**
Create a sense of PURPOSE.	Understand how they contribute and use their natural talents.	Trusted and Informed
PARTICIPATE as a partner.	Included in decisions that impact daily work, given the freedom to play to their strengths.	Valued and Involved
Make PROGRESS possible.	Recognized for progress toward personally meaningful goals.	Recognized and Inspired

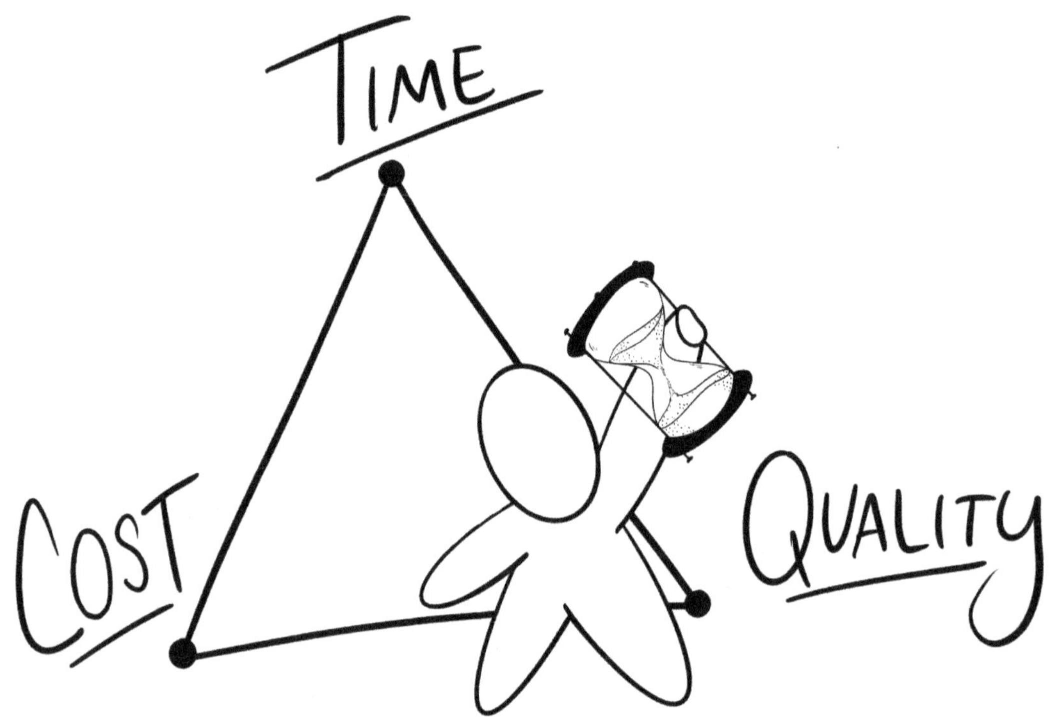

TIME
COST
QUALITY

ENVIRONMENT

Develop your playbook using a common language and frameworks that everyone can access—anytime and anywhere.

Remote and hybrid work arrangements have added a layer of complexity to ensuring everyone is informed, involved, and inspired to do their best work. A plan will help.

People support a world they help create. With only so much sand in the hourglass and mental energy in the day, you have some decisions to make.

One hour spent planning is worth four hours of execution.

– Crawford Greenwalt, DuPont

Planning allows you to be more proactive and intentional in your communication strategies. Hardwired for safety and survival, human beings have reaction as their default setting to external circumstances. Thankfully, you can choose to respond instead of react when you have a plan.

In his 2021 article, "The Difference Between Reacting and Responding," Jim Taylor poses this question, *"Would you rather **react** or **respond** to a situation? The Latin root of react is "back, to do, perform." The key takeaway is that you are taking action back at someone or something. In contrast, the Latin root of respond is "back, answer." The key takeaway is that you are answering back to someone or something, usually in words.*

The Choice Is Yours: React or Respond

As a manager, the choice is yours to react, performing the work yourself, or respond by informing and involving others to do their part. Decisions to do it yourself come from the need to control or self-protect. Decisions to include others create opportunities for growth and development for all.

As a guide on the side, instead of the sage on the stage, it takes courage and humility to share control, putting your faith in the contribution of others, but the result is a game-changer.

THE PARTICIPATION PLAN

YOU HAVE ARRIVED AT DECISION POINT

It's time to turn your thoughts and feelings about the world of work into actions you are willing to take to make work better for all. Whether you plan to create a simple word document, a slide deck, or a webpage to share with your team, the following pages will guide you step by step through the process.

Using what you have discovered about your relationships with the business and those you lead, decide what you want to do differently or improve in your organizational, team, and individual conversations to create more meaningful work.

Smart managers know you reap what you sow.

The seeds of clarity, alignment, and support appear as behaviors on the following pages. The choice is yours to accept, modify, and adapt them to meet your needs.

MEANING-MAKING: Stories We Tell Ourselves About What Is Happening and Why

CONTEXT: Meet people where they are.

What is happening in the workplace today?

Based on your experience, what do these changes mean to you?

OUTCOMES: Define expected outcomes for the future.

What is the gap between current conditions and desired future performance?

What needs to change for managers to close the gap?

DECISION-MAKING: Stories That Determine What We Are Willing To Do as a Result

RELATIONSHIPS: Give everyone a role to play.

What would these changes look like and sound like for you to create opportunities for meaningful participation?

ENVIRONMENT: Determine what resources and conditions are needed.

What would you need to succeed if you were in their shoes?

What barriers or obstacles exist?

MEANING-MAKING = thoughts and beliefs about what change is needed (head and heart).

DECISION-MAKING = a personal choice to act based on the current conditions (guts).

1. CREATE A SENSE OF PURPOSE

Everyone should know and understand what the business needs, why their job exists, and how they contribute their talents and gifts.

Make Organizational Conversations Meaningful

What is the purpose of these coversations?

A well-articulated mission statement or vision can serve as a north star, providing clarity and focus in a sea of competing demands. They allow individuals to be a part of something bigger than themselves and believe their contributions matter.

Being prepared with the history of the organization, its structure, and values saves you time and effort in onboarding a new employee or refocusing the efforts of a team that may have strayed off track. Tracing projects back to why they are needed to fulfill the mission is like having a reset button for managing priorities.

Why are these conversations needed?

When change happens in the organization, everyone wants to be informed and trusted with the most accurate and timely information. New product launches, closing a division or location, and systemwide process modifications are just a few examples of information individuals would prefer to hear first from their manager than the internet, a neighbor, or a customer who appears more knowledgeable than the employee.

What opportunities exist for participation in these conversations?

Managing from the middle, you have little input to these decisions, yet you can gain observations and feedback by asking employees questions like:

- What words or phrases stood out for you in this announcement?
- What was your initial reaction?
- What impact, if any, do you believe that may have on our team?

To complete this section of the playbook:

TABLE 5. INFORMED AND TRUSTED	
As a Strategy Enabler	**As an Environment Creator**
Recount the history of the organization accurately, in your own words.	Offer personal stories and examples of the values reflected in your decisions.
Explain the values and principles that guide daily decisions and actions.	Use analogies, demonstrations, exhibits, and statistics to make key points memorable.
Describe the organizational structure and how individual roles and goals support the mission.	Offer personal examples of how you came to work here and why you are proud to lead this team.

- ☐ The first slide is a snapshot of what is included in the PURPOSE section.
- ☐ In two to three paragraphs describe how your company was founded. In your own words, highlight key points that will be significant to the work of your team.
- ☐ Yes, employees may have heard this story at orientation, amid all the benefits paperwork and company policies. Putting this story in your own words represents an important step in relationship building, especially those in remote or hybrid settings.
- ☐ You can link to other company resources for those who want to learn more.

ACTION ITEMS

- ☐
- ☐
- ☐
- ☐

PURPOSE
We make a difference to the organization.

To **create a sense of purpose**, *this section will answer the following questions:*

- ❏ Looking back, where have we been as an organization?
- ❏ Looking ahead, what changes are happening in our industry?

- ❏ What makes us unique, guiding our decisions?
- ❏ How does our team contribute to results?

- ❏ What does working for this organization means to me?

Where did it all begin?

- ❏ Who was the founder of our organization?
- ❏ What was happening in the world at the time it was founded?
- ❏ What customer need did it fill that made this organization unique?

- ☐ You might consider recent news articles, awards, or web pages to help you tell this story, again in your own words.

ACTION ITEMS

- ☐
- ☐
- ☐
- ☐

Mission. Vision. Values

- ❏ What is our mission?
- ❏ What is the vision for the future?
- ❏ What values guide our decisions?
- ❏ What is our competitive advantage today?

- ☐ Be as specific as possible about whether your team increases revenue production or decreases expenses, directly or indirectly. You can refer to **Table 2. Business Needs on page 31** for support.
- ☐ You may combine these questions into one declarative statement or create a slide for each. Keep your responses brief and to the point.

ACTION ITEMS

- ☐
- ☐
- ☐
- ☐

How does our team add value?

- ❑ How is our organization structured?
- ❑ What is the purpose of our team?
- ❑ How is our performance measured?
- ❑ What would be missing if we didn't exist?

Genuine connection creates change.

—Nancy Duarte, Resonate (2010)

Ideas and Actions to Consider:
- Advances in technology have given us many ways to communicate, yet behind every post, email, tweet, call, or instant message is the desire to connect.
- In a world in which change is constant and complex, the anchor is your ability to connect in a grounded, relevant, genuine way. You set the example for Meaning-Making and build a foundation for trust.

ACTION ITEMS

- ☐
- ☐
- ☐
- ☐

What does this mean to me?

- ☐ I came to work here in (date) _________________.
- ☐ I decided to go to work here because _____________.

- ☐ As the manager of this team, I'm proud of _________________.
- ☐ One thing I enjoy most about my job is _________________.
- ☐ One thing I find challenging is _________________________.

Ideas and Actions to Consider:

- ☐ Share two or three specific examples of team accomplishments, noting the individual, what they did, and what impact it had.
- ☐ Update these examples quarterly to recognize outstanding accomplishments and provide clear examples of progress for individuals and the business.

ACTION ITEMS

- ☐
- ☐
- ☐
- ☐

We make a difference.

❑ Highlights for this quarter include:

Share two or three specific examples of team accomplishments, noting who, did what, and the impact.

2. PARTICIPATE AS A PARTNER

Everyone should be able to use and apply the information they are given to make better decisions that directly affect their work and give them the freedom to play to their strengths with others.

Make Team Conversations Meaningful

What is the purpose of these conversations?

Teams translate business directives into action plans within the hierarchy, systems, and processes designed for organizational efficiency and effectiveness. Managers guide the discussion of shared goals and objectives with others to help everyone stay on track. Participating in the decisions needed to organize efforts, timelines, and resources allows individuals to freely choose to support those decisions with the freedom to do their best work.

Why are these conversations needed?

These conversations are needed to align team members' time, effort, and resources to achieve a shared objective. These meetings answer the following questions:

- ☐ Who?
- ☐ Will do what?
- ☐ By when?
- ☐ How will we measure results?

What opportunities exist for participation in these conversations?

As the manager, you are responsible for bringing the facts and data to establish the purpose of the meeting, a process for how team members will participate, and the progress to be made when results are met.

Those closest to the assignments answer the questions listed above based on their talents, experience, availability, and conditions to do their best work.

To complete this section of the playbook:

TABLE 6. CONTEXT AND OUTCOMES	
As a Strategy Enabler	**As an Environment Creator**
Design meetings with a specific outcome stated in 10 words or less.	Determine the best framework for structuring the conversation to allow for multiple, even competing, points of view and input.
Align meeting outcomes to the purpose and direction of the organization.	Give everyone a role to play in the conversation.
Communicate logistics and time commitments in advance, sharing reports or other materials needed.	Close the meeting by clarifying assignments and timelines and recognizing any important individual contributions to the meeting.

- The first slide is a snapshot of what is included in the PARTICIPATION section.
- The purpose of beginning a meeting by asking how it will move the business forward is to provide context. In Latin, contexere is "to weave or join together." Context refers to the environment or setting in which something exists.
- Business challenges provide many opportunities for learning and growth when you consider what individuals do to meet these challenges.

ACTION ITEMS

-
-
-
-

PARTICIPATION

We work together as a team.

To **participate as partners**, *this section provides a framework for agreements in how we meet:*

- ❑ We begin with a purpose.
- ❑ We focus on outcomes.
- ❑ Everyone prepares to contribute.
- ❑ Everyone participates.
- ❑ Everyone's time is valued.

We begin with a purpose.

We begin every business meeting by asking:
- ❑ In what ways will this conversation move our business forward?
- ❑ In what ways does this business challenge provide opportunities for growth?

- The most motivating factor for individuals at work is making progress toward meaning-ful goals. Knowing at the beginning of a meeting that something will be accomplished for their investment of time and energy is more motivating than a meeting agenda.
- In the 1950s, Benjamin Bloom wanted to improve communication between educa-tors on the design of curricula for students. He classified student learning objectives in three key areas, moving from low- to high-level objectives, improving consistency for results.

Bloom's work can improve your communication for clarity and accountability. Download a copy at https://www.bcit.ca/files/ltc/pdf/ja_learningoutcomes.pdf

ACTION ITEMS

- ☐
- ☐
- ☐
- ☐

Every meeting has an outcome.

To schedule a meeting with 2 or more people, the announcement must include:
In 10 words or less, what will be different when this meeting is over?

Examples: (note, they all start with a verb)
- ❏ **Select** *a topic for the upcoming conference.*
- ❏ **Review** *the XYZ proposal for management recommendations.*
- ❏ **Prepare** *a short presentation for the project update meeting.*

- ☐ After opening the meeting with the desired outcome, tell everyone what to be listening for to ensure more meaningful participation.
- ☐ **Table 7.** Roles and Expectations offer examples, based on the need.

TABLE 7. ROLES AND EXPECTATIONS	
Your Role	**Their Role**
CLARITY Present the facts with concrete examples. You know what you said. You don't know what they heard.	**FACTS** Listen for the specific steps to . . . Who can recall them without hesitation? **OPINIONS** What are your thoughts about. . . ?
ALIGNMENT Invite input and respect multiple points of view. You know how you would do it. You don't know if there is a better, faster, or more efficient way.	**APPLICATION** What has worked in the past on . . . ? Who has an idea about . . . ? **USAGE** How will you use this information to . . . ? What's missing?
INDIVIDUAL SUPPORT Provide feedback, and call out progress. You know if the performance was satisfactory. You don't know if it was satisfying or meaningful to team members.	**FUTURE-FOCUSED** What if we are asked to repeat this? What would you do differently? **PERSONAL MEANING** In what ways does this support your long-term goals? What was this experience like for you?

ACTION ITEMS

- ☐
- ☐
- ☐
- ☐

Everyone prepares to contribute.

To make the best decisions possible as a team and learn from the experience of others we prepare to contribute.

Examples:

- ❏ Listen for **facts** and details that require clarification.
- ❏ Offer **opinions** and insights to explore a topic more thoroughly.
- ❏ Offer **examples** of processes or procedures that worked in the past.
- ❏ Explain the **application** of new information to improve results.

How many times have you participated in a conversation during which:
- too much time was wasted trying to identify the real issue?
- it was all talk about the work, but no real work happened?
- you were asked for your opinion or ideas but were not given time to think or to share them appropriately?

☐ A safe, healthy exchange of ideas requires structure. It's not enough to show up with the right outcome statement and expect results. For participation to be meaningful, individuals want to contribute their experiences and ideas to the conversation.

☐ Despite the abundance of meeting templates and formats, many focus primarily on mechanics. RACI, DIA, and other structures are designed to manage and monitor project status and shared accountability.

☐ These formats lack the participation opportunities individuals need for a robust idea exchange or sharing of relevant work experience. The Axelrod Group's Meeting Canoe is one example of a meeting structure designed to connect people to each other and the work.

☐ Identify a few templates that work for your team and post them here for everyone to review.

ACTION ITEMS

☐

☐

☐

☐

Everyone participates.

Structure creates freedom.

The First 5-minutes

Every meeting begins with check-in for all participants. The format can vary, but the goal is meaningful participation. (Cameras are on if online and available)

The Format

Following check-in, the meeting begins with a purpose, a process, and a way to measure progress.

The Final 5-minutes

Before the meeting ends, the results are summarized, and the next actions are reviewed and assigned.

- ☐ The best way to establish guidelines and group norms is to ask the team members to develop their list. This is particularly important in hybrid and alternate work arrangements. Once established, they own the outcome.

ACTION ITEMS

- ☐
- ☐
- ☐
- ☐

Everyone's time is valuable.

Given the amount of time we spend at work, we practice the following guidelines
to create a supportive, informative community of partners:

1.

2.

3.

4.

5.

6.

7.

3. MAKE PROGRESS POSSIBLE

Everyone should be able to continuously evaluate and improve results that move the business forward and grow their talents and skills.

Make Individual Conversations Meaningful

What is the purpose of these conversations?

We have all heard we are born with gifts and natural talent, yet we're often unsure exactly what they are or how to describe them. Our estimate of our abilities is not always accurate, and sometimes the expectations of others confuse the matter even more. Helping others through observation and feedback gives individuals language to identify and share their talents with others.

Why are these conversations needed?

Even when individuals know what is expected and believe they have what they need to accomplish the task, they may lack the courage to move forward. Coach individuals to identify these issues and remove barriers to help them think for themselves and find the resources to turn fear and doubt into confident action.

Stress and conflict often occur in the workplace when we don't know how to ask for what we need or work with others whose approach is different from ours. Giving everyone the language they need to know what they are naturally good at and how they can contribute to a project or task provides the freedom to do their best work.

What opportunities exist for participation in these conversations?

Constructive, person-centered feedback is a gift. Many organizations have eliminated the formal midyear and end-of-year performance reviews, opting for continuous and more meaningful feedback. Establish 1:1 time for these conversations at least once a quarter.

To complete this section of the playbook:

TABLE 8. TALENT AND DEVELOPMENT	
As a Strategy Enabler	**As an Environment Creator**
Provide feedback based on observations, naming progress toward goals and areas for improvement.	Ask questions to learn more about the individual's background, experience, and goals for the future.
Track progress over time to document successes and provide evidence of growth in personal and professional goals.	Ask questions to prompt self-generated insights, like "what are your concerns, or doubts? What is getting in the way?"
Determine advanced learning or promotion opportunities to develop skills.	Recall and repeats stories, names, and contributions from previous interactions.

Ideas and Actions to Consider:

- The first slide is a snapshot of what is included in the PROGRESS section.
- Work anniversaries are an example of celebrating moments that matter. A brief note or call to recognize the day and their contributions takes little time and effort yet means a great deal to the individual.
- In hybrid or deskless work environments, managers must be more intentional about making these connections. Virtual coffee breaks or morning check-ins can offer individuals the attention and support they deserve.

ACTION ITEMS

- ☐
- ☐
- ☐
- ☐

PROGRESS

We grow and develop our natural talent and skills.

*To **make progress possible**, in this section set expectations for exploring natural talents and understanding individual long-term goals and objectives.*

- ❑ Celebrate employee moments that matter.
- ❑ Identify natural talent.
- ❑ Determine how to contribute it in the most effective, efficient way.
- ❑ Measure and monitor progress toward personally meaningful goals.

We celebrate moments that matter.

Orientation

Every new employee has a 30/60/90-day plan to meet the team, become familiar with team processes and procedures, and contribute fresh insights and ideas to improve workflow.

Career Development

Everyone has a 1:1 meeting with their manager monthly for a minimum of 30 minutes to discuss progress on current projects, what is most challenging, and what is most engaging about the work. The conversation is future-focused.

Advancement

Long-term goals are revisited quarterly to recognize progress and the next steps.

Ask the following questions of every individual and observe their progress. Help them discover what their skills look like in action and the impact:

- What about your work motivates you the most?
- What kinds of things do you do where the time passes quickly and the task is engaging?
- What fuels your energy?
- When others call you for help, what are they typically asking you for?
- What do you find most challenging? What drains your energy during the day?
- Where do you believe you make the greatest contribution, and why?
- What does progress look like to you?

ACTION ITEMS

-
-
-
-

Identify natural talent.

The following questions provide evidence and clues to natural talent and instincts:

1. What about your work motivates you the most?
2. What kinds of things are you doing when time passes quickly and the task is engaging?
3. What fuels your energy? What drains your energy during the day?
4. When others call you for help, what are they typically asking you for?
5. Where do you believe you make the greatest contribution, and why?

Meaning-Making and Your Power to Choose

☐ As a manager, listen for the meaning-making when someone is hesitating to act. Listen to the stories they are telling themselves and help them see they have the resources within, using the prompts below.

TABLE 9. AVOID RISK AND CREATE REWARD	
AVOID RISK	**CREATE REWARD**
Fear-Based Stories	**Faith-Based Stories**
Doubt – I don't know if I can.	Confidence – I can take the next step.
Discouragement – it probably won't work.	Encouragement – I'll ask ____for help.
Distraction – I can't do it because…	Focus – One thing I can focus on is…
Defeat – why bother?	Past Success – I've done this before.
Delay – now isn't a good time, so I'll do it later.	Action - What I can do now is…

ACTION ITEMS

☐

☐

☐

☐

Your Power to Choose

TABLE 9.	
AVOID RISK	**CREATE REWARD**
Fear-Based Stories	Faith-Based Stories
Doubt – I don't know if I can.	Confidence – I can take the next step.
Discouragement – it probably won't work.	Encouragement – I'll ask _____ for help.
Distraction – I can't do it because…	Focus – One thing I can focus on is…
Defeat – why bother?	Past Success – I've done this before.
Delay – now isn't a good time, so I'll do it later.	Action – What I can do now is…

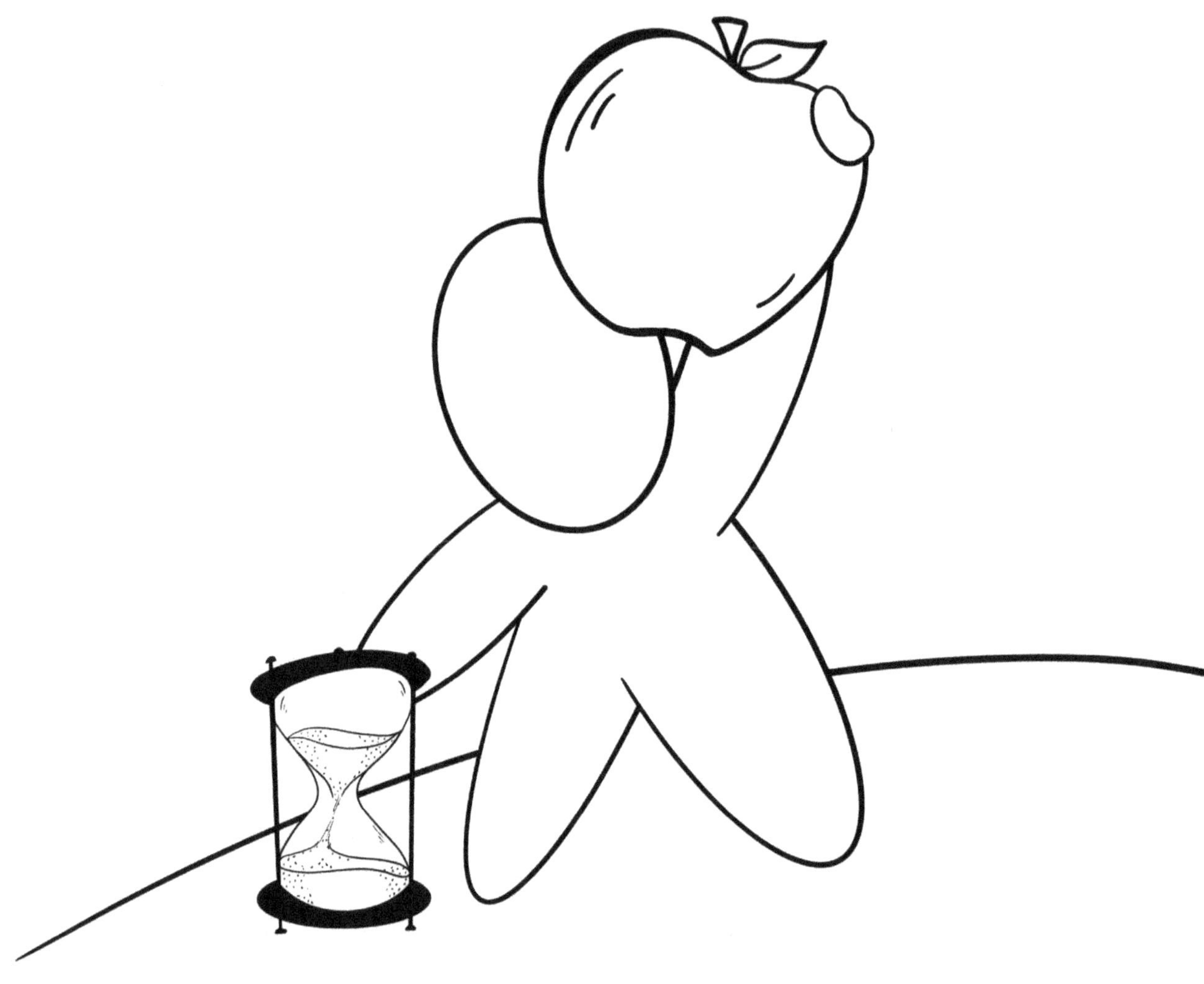

If you know something must change, then know that it is you who must change it.

– Susan Scott, Fierce Conversations (2002)

References

Josh Bersin, "Business Trends: Work Is Still Work," updated January 5, 2021, https://joshbersin.com/2021/01/work-is-still-work/.

Larry Bossidy and Ram Charan, *Execution: The Discipline of Getting Things Done* (New York: Crown Book, 2002).

Nicholas Carr, *The Shallows: What the Internet Is Doing to Our Brains* (New York: Norton, 2020).

Nancy Duarte, *DataStory*: *Explain Data and Inspire Action Through Story* (Oakton, VA: Ideapress, 2019).

Nancy Duarte, *Resonate: Present Visual Stories That Transform Audiences* (Hoboken, NJ: Wiley, 2010).

Ronald C. Eng, ed., *Mountaineering: The Freedom of the Hills*, 8th ed. (Seattle, WA: Mountaineers Books, 2010).

Ferdinand Fournies, *Why Employees Don't Do What They Are Supposed to Do and What to Do About It* (New York: McGraw-Hill, 2007).

Alison King, "From Sage on the Stage to Guide on the Side," *College Teaching* 41, no. 1 (1993): 30–35.

Malcolm Knowles, *The Adult Learner: A Neglected Species* (Houston, TX: Gulf Publishing, 1973).

Kathy Kolbe, *The Conative Connection: Uncovering the Link Between Who You Are and How You Perform* (n.p.: Kolbe, 1989).

Abraham Maslow, Deborah Stephens, and Gary Heil, *Maslow on Management* (New York: Wiley, 1998).

Microsoft, "Work Trend Index Special Report: Hybrid Work Is Just Work. Are We Doing It Wrong?," September 22, 2022, https://www.microsoft.com/en-us/worklab/work-trend-index/.

Vicek H. Murthy M.D., M.B.A., *The U.S. Surgeon General's Framework for Workplace Mental Health and Well-Being* (Washington, DC: Public Health Service, Office of the U.S. Surgeon General, 2022), https://www.hhs.gov/surgeongeneral/priorities/workplace-well-being/index.html.

Daniel Pink, *Drive: The Surprising Truth About What Motivates Us* (New York: Riverhead Books 2011).

Fran Rees, *How to Lead Work Teams: Facilitation Skills* (San Francisco: Jossey-Bass, 1991).

Susan Scott, *Fierce Conversations: Achieving Success at Work and in Life, One Conversation at a Time* (New York: New American Library, 2017).

Brian Stanfield, ed., *The Art of Focused Conversation: 100 Ways to Access Group Wisdom in the Workplace* (British Columbia, Canada: New Society Publishers, 2009).